Making Success A Reality

Success Journal

Created by Melissa S. Myers

Copyright © Melissa S. Myers, 2020

Cover image: © Danny Media

ISBN-13: 9780578750682

Publisher's Note

Printed and bound in the United States of America. All rights reserved. No part of this book may be reproduced or transmitted in any form or by any means, electronic or mechanical, including photocopying, recording, or by any information storage and retrieval system except by a reviewer who may quote brief passages in a review to be printed in a magazine, newspaper, or on the Web without permission in writing from Melissa S. Myers.

Although the author and publisher have made every effort to ensure the accuracy and completeness of information contained in this book, we assume no responsibility for errors, inaccuracies, omissions, or any inconsistency herein. The advice and strategies contained herein may not be suitable for your situation. You should consult with a professional where appropriate. Neither the publisher nor the author shall be liable for damages arising from here.

For: God

God: "Don't you trust me?"

Me: "Yes, of course I do."

Contents

Habakkuk 2:2-4 KJV 1
Journal Purpose 2
Prayer 3
The Formula of Life 4
You 6
Toxic Traits 7
Reflection: The present & the future prayer 8
Struggles 9
Achievements 10
Self-Care 11
Daily Self Care 12
Finances 15
Bill 16
Desires 18
Goals 20
Loved Ones 22
Who do you want to be successful for? 23
Who have you lost in your life that
you want to make proud 24
The Circle 26
Friends 27
Spouse/Significant other/Potential 28
Business Connections 29

Networking Events 30
No New Friends 33
Words from the Author 35
Journal 36
Affirmations 37
About the Author 397

Habakkuk 2:2-4 KJV

"And the LORD answered me, and said, Write the vision, and make it plain upon tables, that he may run that readeth it. For the vision is yet for an appointed time, but at the end it shall speak, and not lie: though it tarry, wait for it; because it will surely come, it will not tarry. Behold, his soul which is lifted up is not upright in him: but the just shall live by his faith."

Journal Purpose

To align success in your life, you must have a clear outlook into what path you are currently on. This journal will allow you to dig deep and ask yourself those hard questions to make you think about the areas in our lives we tend to ignore. We often overlook areas that are important when moving towards our goals to be successful. We can't move forward in life if we haven't healed from our past, have the lack of strength in our social circle, and fail to take an honest look at ourselves to create the desire to change. At times we are quick to point the finger at others and blame them for our shortcomings, but this journal will take the power from those individuals and place that power in your hands. Once you heal and overcome the roadblocks you've faced, you are on the journey to success. This journal is private and is a personal look into your life. This is not a journal to be viewed by anyone as it creates a declaration between you and GOD to live a life of abundance and control.

Father, I come to you as humble as I know how. I pray the individual that is completing this journal will do so without fear. Speak to this individual as I ask that you provide guidance during this task. I pray that this journal opens the eyes, the mind, as well as the spirit to recognize what and who is around them. I pray completing this journal heals their wounds, repairs their damaged heart, and they begin to hear you clearly as they take upon this new journey in their life. I count it as done. In Jesus name…Amen.

In life, there are certain things we require that will lead us to prosperity. We can't achieve one without the other. If we try to speed up our life journey we will encounter potholes on the highway of our lives. We have to set a foundation for ourselves, whether it is our belief, health, or family; whatever we decide is most important in our journey. Without creating our formula for our lives, we will continue to hydroplane until we choose to slow down and focus.

For Arman

Instructions: In the circle, write what you feel is needed for you to prosper in life. It can be something as small but mighty as "Positivity." This will be used as your guide.

You

Many times, it has been said not to look in the rearview mirror as you move forward in life; I can agree with that to a certain aspect. On the other hand, there are times where we have to reflect on where we have been to realize how far we have come. To see how GOD has pulled us out of situations that could have had us in a hole that couldn't have gotten ourselves out of. It is easy to get down in our current situations, but we have to look back and realize the many obstacles we have overcome. This section will allow you to take a hard look at yourself. On the other hand, we can't expect a change in our lives, if we don't achieve change within ourselves. Like mentioned previously, it is easy to point the fingers at everyone else, but there are times where we have to point the finger at ourselves.

MAKING SUCCESS A REALITY

Instructions: In this section, you will be honest about the toxic traits that you possess. You will list your toxic traits, how it affects your life, and what you can do to change that trait. Having toxic energy will affect the relationships around you and hinder you from true success and happiness.

Toxic	How is it affecting	How can you change it?

Reflection: The present & the future prayer

Instructions: In this exercise, reflect on various areas of your life. It could be your career, love life, family, etc. Whatever it is, write it down. Compare where you were then to where you are now; this will allow you to observe if there has been any progress. Lastly, what you would like to accomplish in that area.

Where have you been?	Where are you now?	What goals do you want to accomplish?

MAKING SUCCESS A REALITY

Struggles

Instructions: In each diagram, write the following: What is your struggle? What caused the struggle? How can you overcome this struggle? Don't forget to include any childhood struggles.

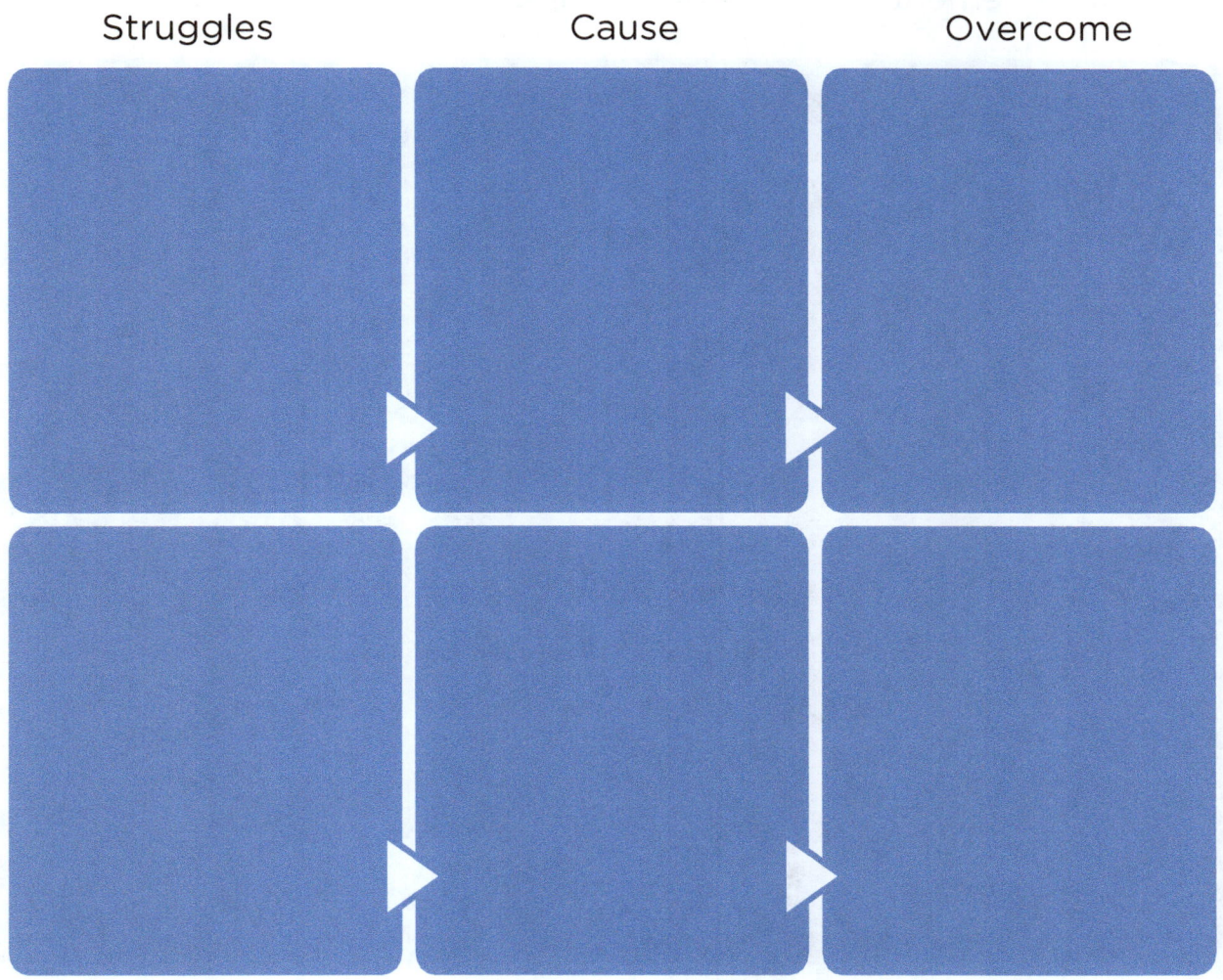

9

MAKING SUCCESS A REALITY

Instructions: In each diagram, write the following: What are your achievements? Did anyone help you (also identify if they are still in your life)? How has this achievement bettered your life?

Achievements	Person Helped?	How is life Better

Self-Care

Many of us work, take care of our families, and even others in the community. This creates a large amount of responsibility for us daily. We spend so much time taking care of others, we forget to take care of ourselves. The failure of self-care can bring many issues to your life, such as getting sick more often and feelings of isolation or depression, just to name a few. While the task of self-care seems mundane or not an important factor in our life, practicing self-care creates the ability to become more focused and to have healthy relationships. As life becomes unpredictable with what can be thrown at us, maintaining adequate self-care will mentally prepare you for the inevitable.

Daily Self Care

Instructions: There are various methods of self-care. Here are 50 ways to achieve self-care. Review them and practice at least once daily. Regular self-care will give you control over your life as well as your health. You will find your method of practicing selfcare and will notice the mental and physical improvement.

Build a Healthy Foundation

1. Get enough sleep and do your best to keep a consistent sleep schedule
2. Eat a balanced diet and include fruits and vegetables
3. Drink at least 8 glasses of water

Avoid Stress

4. Avoid triggers
5. Take breaks from your computer, phone, or social media
6. Learn to say NO. (It's ok to say no if you don't want to or aren't able to do something at the moment. Taking on too many commitments can put extra pressure on yourself and cause more stress.)

Feeling Low on Energy? (Even Small Steps Matter)

7. Wash your face, take a shower if you can
8. Put on clean, comfortable clothes
9. Eat something and drink water — if you're able to make your favorite snack or order takeout
10. Read, watch your favorite shows or movies, and try not to feel guilty about not being productive

Relax

11. Play video games
12. Watch your favorite tv show
13. Rent a movie
14. Play Sudoku or other puzzle games
15. Listen to music
16. Use scented candles or diffuse essential oils
17. Meditate
18. Take a bubble bath or shower and use your favorite shampoo/conditioner, body wash, and lotion
19. Read a book

Get Active

20. Do some simple stretches to get your blood moving
21. Go for a walk
22. Go to a yoga class or try yoga videos at home
23. Try other fitness classes like water aerobics or kickboxing, many gyms offer classes for a wide range of athletic abilities
24. Dance
25. Join a community sports team like softball or kickball

Get Outside

26. Go for a short walk
27. Ride your bike, skateboard, or rollerblade
28. Have lunch in the park
29. Go to the beach
30. Go for a hike

Social Activities

31. Have dinner or coffee with friends
32. Text, call, or Skype with a friend
33. Join an online community to connect with others
34. Go to a movie with a friend
35. Visit with your family
36. Play board games with friends or family
37. Plan a trip with friends

Creative Outlets

38. Drawing
39. Writing
40. Adult coloring books
41. Painting
42. Try a DIY (Do It Yourself) project
43. Cooking
44. Baking
45. Work on anything that inspires you

Treat Yourself

46. Get a manicure or pedicure
47. Give yourself a manicure or have your friend give you one
48. Get a massage
49. Buy something small for yourself
50. Eat your favorite meal or dessert

Finances

Money is such an important factor when wanting to achieve success. Not having enough money is a common reason used for not achieving our goals. We use the excuse that we have bills, dependents, and lack of time because of work that prevents us from achieving our goals. Sometimes a little restructuring in your spending goes a long way. There is a saying that sometimes you have to take a step back to move forward. Making the sacrifice now will bring a future of financial freedom.

Bill

Instructions: Time to open your checkbook or your online account and take a closer look at your spending. List every bill that you have, every amount you spend on eating out or any guilty pleasure. List how much you spend on the item monthly. Is it required for you to have it? Can you cut back or do without? Most importantly, how much can you save on this item? In the end, add the total amount you can save monthly.

MAKING SUCCESS A REALITY

Current Bills	How Much?	Required?	Cut Back/Do Without?	How much can you save?
			Total Saved	

Desires

Instructions: If money wasn't a factor, what do you want? I don't care how big it is, because you're not going to put GOD in a box as we are going to believe GOD for the impossible. So, write down your desires, how much will it cost, and most importantly, will this be an investment to bring in an additional income? If so, how much? For example: Let's say you want to purchase a new vehicle. Can that new vehicle bring in a stream of income, such as becoming an Uber driver or making deliveries? Specify how you plan to use that investment to bring in additional income if so.

MAKING SUCCESS A REALITY

Desire _____	**Desire** _____
Cost _____	Cost _____
Invest _____	Invest _____
Income _____	Income _____
Desire _____	**Desire** _____
Cost _____	Cost _____
Invest _____	Invest _____
Income _____	Income _____
Desire _____	**Desire** _____
Cost _____	Cost _____
Invest _____	Invest _____
Income _____	Income _____

Goals

Instructions: From the "Reflection: the Present and the Future" and the "Desires" exercise, transfer your goals and your desires in the chart below. You will then list what the requirements are to achieve this goal. Set a **REALISTIC** deadline to achieve them by. Be prepared for any foreseen roadblocks that may affect your goal deadline, but don't use it as an excuse not to get your goal achieved.

Goal	Goal Requirements	Date to Accomplish	Roadblocks?
Goal	Goal Requirements	Date to Accomplish	Roadblocks?

MAKING SUCCESS A REALITY

Goal	Goal Requirements	Date to Accomplish	Roadblocks?
Goal	Goal Requirements	Date to Accomplish	Roadblocks?
Goal	Goal Requirements	Date to Accomplish	Roadblocks?
Goal	Goal Requirements	Date to Accomplish	Roadblocks?

Loved Ones

There is always some motivation when trying to achieve success. Many times, some individuals motivate us to have the desire to do better. We must dissect if we are moving toward a goal because we are doing it for ourselves, or doing it to please others. The ultimate goal in life is to obtain true happiness. While we may have the desire to be selfless and care for those around us, we must learn to put our happiness first.

Who do you want to be successful for?

Instructions: Place the person's name in your waking life that you want to be successful for in the center and write you are motivated to make this individual happy in the surrounding areas. The object is to observe if your motivation to please this individual would bring happiness to you.

Who have you lost in your life that you want to make proud

Instructions: Many times, we have lost someone we love too soon. We have achieved something in our lives, wishing that we can share that special moment with that individual. Write the person's name on the line below. Then write three life lessons that this individual has taught you, whether directly or indirectly and how these lessons will help achieve your goals.

MAKING SUCCESS A REALITY

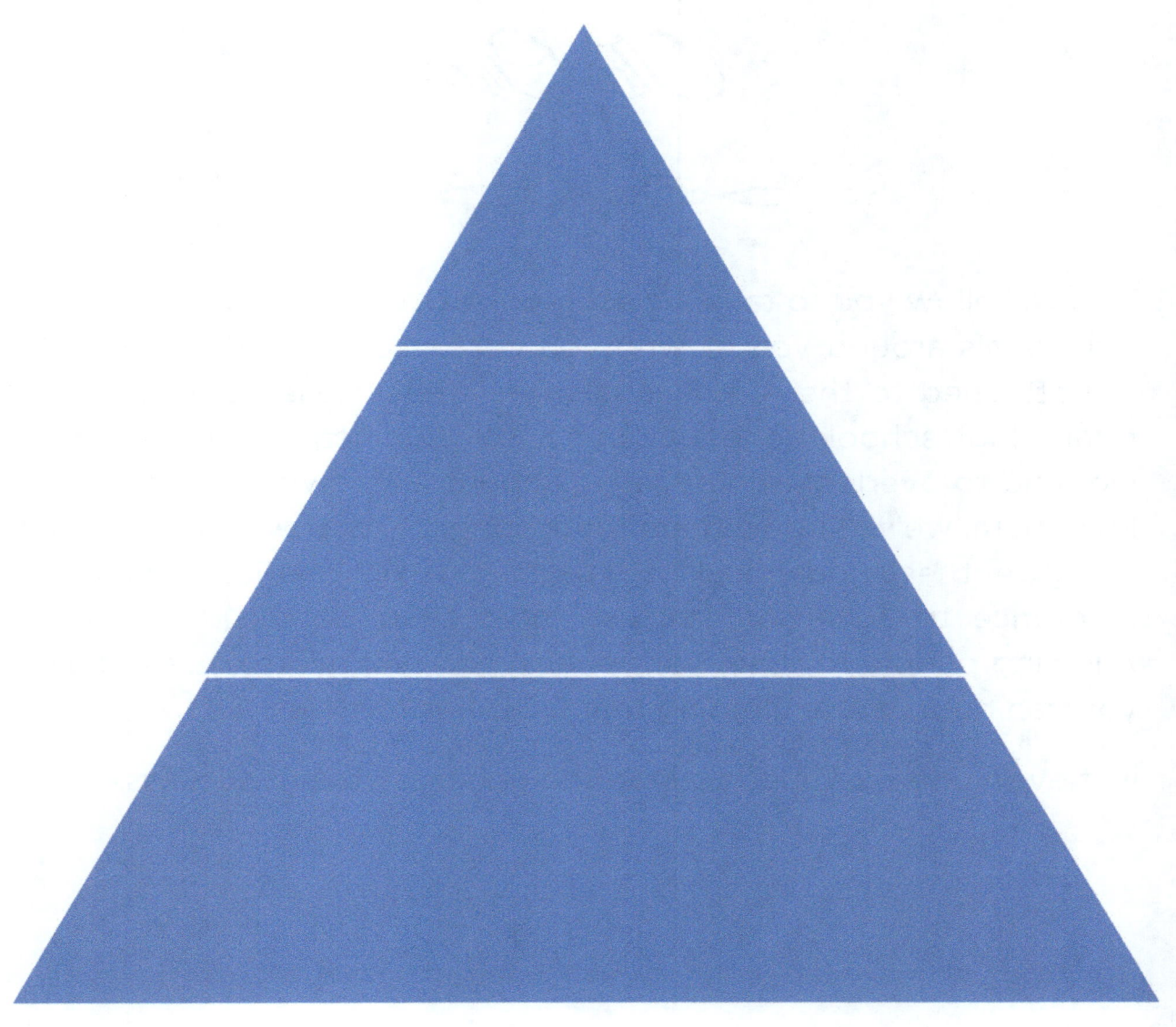

Person's Name

The Circle

This will allow you to take a closer look at your social circle and the individuals around you or who you converse with frequently. We are attached to these individuals for various reasons. It could be family, high school friends; it can be your significant other. At times, we tend to overlook the negatives about an individual because we love them, we've known them for so long, or whatever other reason we give these individuals a "pass." Toxic relationships are a hindrance to achieving success more than we desire to admit. Allowing people to drain your energy, or even worse, pray against you can hold up the blessing that GOD has for you.

Not everyone is entitled to reap the benefits of your success.

MAKING SUCCESS A REALITY

Instructions: Write each of your friend's names in the outer shape. In the inner section, write the following: Why do you consider this individual your friend? How has your friend shown support to you, and how often? Does your friend have a toxic trait? If so, what is it, and how has it affected you?

Spouse/Significant other/Potential

Instructions: In the circle located in the middle of the diagram, write your significant other's name. In each of the surrounding circles write something positive that your significant other contributes to your life and something negative you can do without.

MAKING SUCCESS A REALITY

Business Connections

Instructions: An important factor in achieving success is connecting yourself with subject matter experts to assist you. Write down the name, area of expertise, and contact information of your business connection in the outer diagram. In the inner shape, write down ways the business connection can help you achieve your goals.

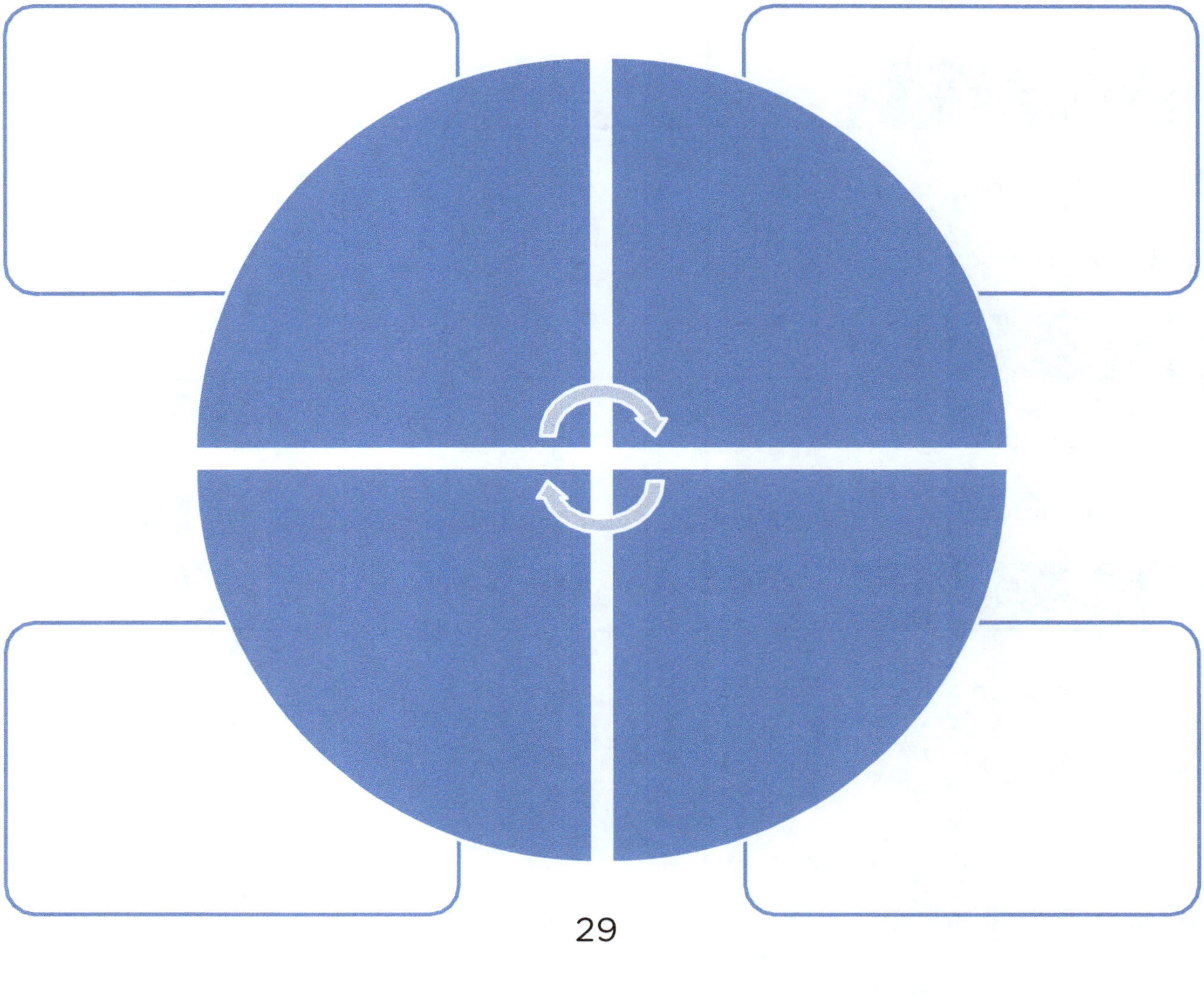

MAKING SUCCESS A REALITY

Networking events are a great way of meeting new individuals that can broaden your connections as well as business opportunities.

Instructions: In this exercise, the goal would be to attend a few networking events. Social media, business chambers, and community events are great resources to learn about various events in your area or virtual events.

Event Name:

Location:

Event Purpose:

Event Name:

Location:

Event Purpose:

Event Name:

Location:

Event Purpose:

MAKING SUCCESS A REALITY

Event Name:

Location:

Event Purpose:

Event Name:

Location:

Event Purpose:

Event Name:

Location:

Event Purpose:

Event Name:

Location:

Event Purpose:

Event Name:

Location:

Event Purpose:

Event Name:

Location:

Event Purpose:

MAKING SUCCESS A REALITY

Event Name:

Location:

Event Purpose:

Event Name:

Location:

Event Purpose:

Event Name:

Location:

Event Purpose:

Event Name:

Location:

Event Purpose:

Event Name:

Location:

Event Purpose:

Event Name:

Location:

Event Purpose:

No New Friends

At times we create the mentality only to be close to those we have known for years, not knowing that could cause us to stunt our growth if we don't expand our circle to new friends. Limiting yourself to the same friends can leave your goals stagnant, and as shocking as it may sound, sometimes, your circle has to be replaced.

Instructions: Meet someone new. This individual can be a new friend or a business connection. Keep in mind if you have a significant other and meet someone of the opposite sex, please be respectful.

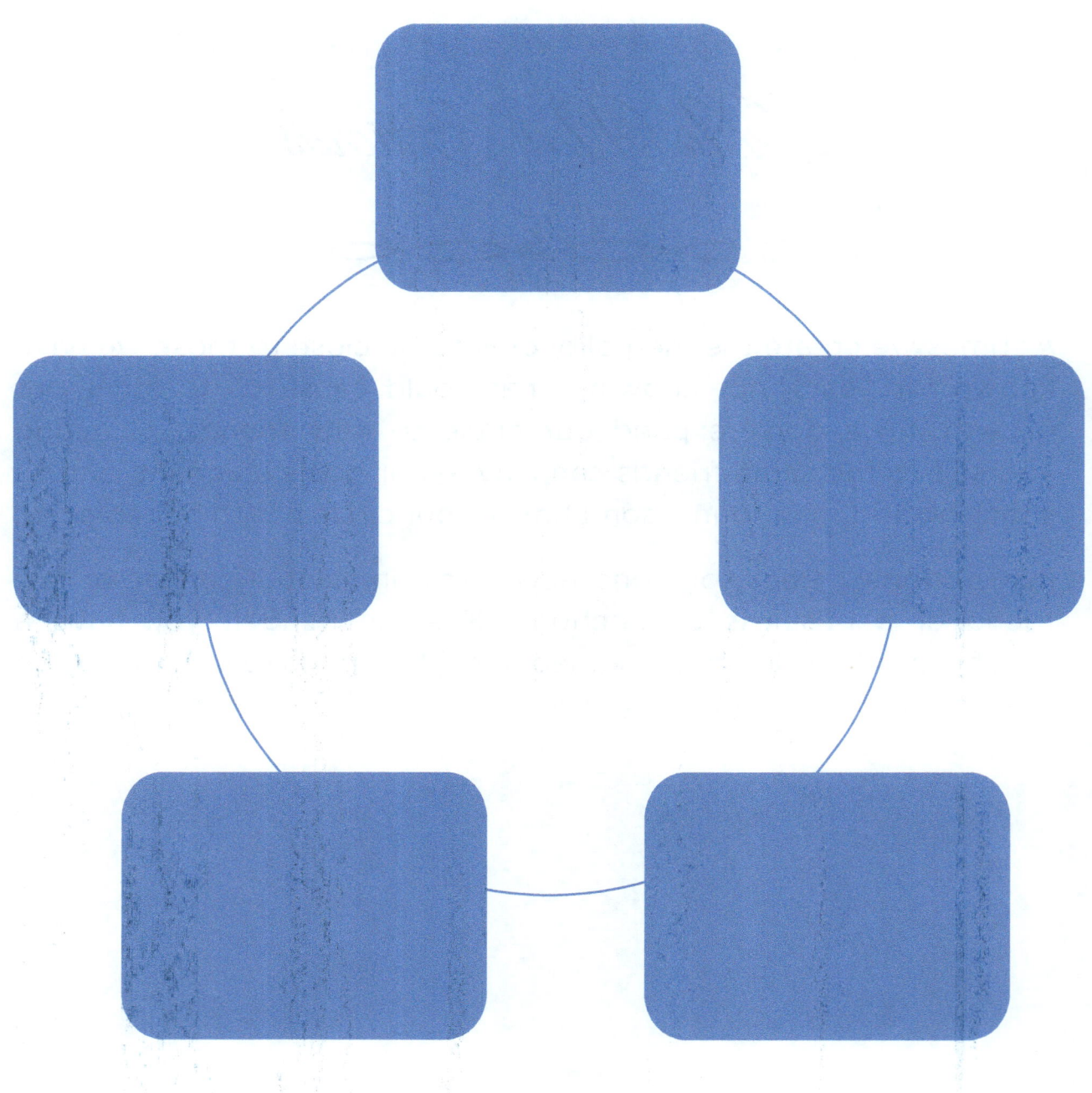

Words from the Author

Sunday, July 12th, 2020 is the day I completed this journal. That morning, I was back and forth about either completing my journal first or cleaning out my closet that I had been putting off for weeks. This closet wasn't just my closet where I kept my clothes, but it is my WAR ROOM. I heard in the spirit that GOD was going to give me something additional to put in my journal. So, I proceeded to clean my closet. This, which started as a physically cleaning, ended up being a spiritual cleansing. When I clean, I think, I process, I solve many situations and come up with ideas. Suddenly the Lord gave me the song, "Your Destiny" By Kevin Levar. I pray it touches you just as much as it touched me.

Melissa S. Myers

Journal

Journaling is a way to express your thoughts, goals, and ideas along with frustrations you may have. Writing these down gives you an outlet to pour out what is on your mind by writing. The ultimate goal is to have a conversation between you and GOD asking for guidance through various trials you may be going through in life. You encounter a newfound success that you are thankful for or a roadblock that you are facing where you need GOD's help to overcome. Whatever it is, write it down. I have journaled and went back to reflect on my writings and reminded myself how far I have come over the years. Journaling will do the same for you.

There is power in the tongue. Be careful what you put out into the atmosphere or the universe. Many of us have heard our grandmothers, mothers, and aunts tell us this growing up. Speaking positivity in our lives is something that we must do, no matter how dire our circumstances. Reciting positive affirmations each morning will set the tone for your day. Even if you knowingly expect a bleak outcome, you would be surprised how GOD will turn a situation around. For example, when you start your day, look into your mirror and state, "I am Brave," "I am Successful," "Today I will have a day of blessings and abundance." Speaking positive affirmations will allow you to be ready to conquer anything that may come your way.

Daily Affirmation_____

Self-Care_____

MAKING SUCCESS A REALITY

Daily Affirmation_____

Self-Care_____

_____

_____

_____

_____

_____

_____

_____

_____

_____

_____

_____

_____

Daily Affirmation_____

Self-Care_____

MAKING SUCCESS A REALITY

Daily Affirmation_____

Self-Care_____

_____

_____

_____

_____

_____

_____

_____

_____

_____

_____

_____

_____

Daily Affirmation_____

Self-Care_____

_____

_____

_____

_____

_____

_____

_____

_____

_____

_____

_____

_____

_____

MAKING SUCCESS A REALITY

Daily Affirmation_____

Self-Care_____

Daily Affirmation_____

Self-Care_____

MAKING SUCCESS A REALITY

Daily Affirmation_____

Self-Care_____

_____

_____

_____

_____

_____

_____

_____

_____

_____

_____

_____

_____

_____

Daily Affirmation_____

Self-Care_____

MAKING SUCCESS A REALITY

Daily Affirmation_____

Self-Care_____

_____

_____

_____

_____

_____

_____

_____

_____

_____

_____

_____

_____

Daily Affirmation_____

Self-Care_____

MAKING SUCCESS A REALITY

Daily Affirmation_____

Self-Care_____

_____

_____

_____

_____

_____

_____

_____

_____

_____

_____

_____

_____

Daily Affirmation_____

Self-Care_____

MAKING SUCCESS A REALITY

Daily Affirmation_____

Self-Care_____

Daily Affirmation_____

Self-Care_____

_____

_____

_____

_____

_____

_____

_____

_____

_____

_____

_____

_____

_____

MAKING SUCCESS A REALITY

Daily Affirmation_____

Self-Care_____

_____

_____

_____

_____

_____

_____

_____

_____

_____

_____

_____

_____

_____

Daily Affirmation_____

Self-Care_____

_____

_____

_____

_____

_____

_____

_____

_____

_____

_____

_____

_____

_____

MAKING SUCCESS A REALITY

Daily Affirmation_____

Self-Care_____

_____

_____

_____

_____

_____

_____

_____

_____

_____

_____

_____

_____

_____

_____

Daily Affirmation_____

Self-Care_____

_____

_____

_____

_____

_____

_____

_____

_____

_____

_____

_____

_____

_____

MAKING SUCCESS A REALITY

Daily Affirmation_____

Self-Care_____

_____

_____

_____

_____

_____

_____

_____

_____

_____

_____

_____

_____

Daily Affirmation_____

Self-Care_____

MAKING SUCCESS A REALITY

Daily Affirmation_____

Self-Care_____

_____

_____

_____

_____

_____

_____

_____

_____

_____

_____

_____

_____

_____

Daily Affirmation_____

Self-Care_____

MAKING SUCCESS A REALITY

Daily Affirmation_____

Self-Care_____

_____

_____

_____

_____

_____

_____

_____

_____

_____

_____

_____

_____

_____

Daily Affirmation_____

Self-Care_____

MAKING SUCCESS A REALITY

Daily Affirmation_____

Self-Care_____

_____

_____

_____

_____

_____

_____

_____

_____

_____

_____

_____

_____

Daily Affirmation_____

Self-Care_____

_____

_____

_____

_____

_____

_____

_____

_____

_____

_____

_____

_____

_____

MAKING SUCCESS A REALITY

Daily Affirmation_____

Self-Care_____

Daily Affirmation_____

Self-Care_____

MAKING SUCCESS A REALITY

Daily Affirmation _____

Self-Care _____

Daily Affirmation_____

Self-Care_____

MAKING SUCCESS A REALITY

Daily Affirmation_____

Self-Care_____

Daily Affirmation_____

Self-Care_____

MAKING SUCCESS A REALITY

Daily Affirmation_____

Self-Care_____

Daily Affirmation_____

Self-Care_____

MAKING SUCCESS A REALITY

Daily Affirmation_____

Self-Care_____

Daily Affirmation_____

Self-Care_____

_____

_____

_____

_____

_____

_____

_____

_____

_____

_____

_____

_____

_____

MAKING SUCCESS A REALITY

Daily Affirmation_____

Self-Care_____

_____

_____

_____

_____

_____

_____

_____

_____

_____

_____

_____

_____

_____

Daily Affirmation_____

Self-Care_____

MAKING SUCCESS A REALITY

Daily Affirmation_____

Self-Care_____

_____

_____

_____

_____

_____

_____

_____

_____

_____

_____

_____

_____

_____

Daily Affirmation_____

Self-Care_____

_____

_____

_____

_____

_____

_____

_____

_____

_____

_____

_____

_____

_____

MAKING SUCCESS A REALITY

Daily Affirmation_____

Self-Care_____

Daily Affirmation_____

Self-Care_____

MAKING SUCCESS A REALITY

Daily Affirmation_____

Self-Care_____

_____

_____

_____

_____

_____

_____

_____

_____

_____

_____

_____

_____

_____

Daily Affirmation_____

Self-Care_____

MAKING SUCCESS A REALITY

Daily Affirmation_____

Self-Care_____

Daily Affirmation_____

Self-Care_____

MAKING SUCCESS A REALITY

Daily Affirmation_____

Self-Care_____

_____

_____

_____

_____

_____

_____

_____

_____

_____

_____

_____

_____

Daily Affirmation_____

Self-Care_____

MAKING SUCCESS A REALITY

Daily Affirmation_____

Self-Care_____

_____

_____

_____

_____

_____

_____

_____

_____

_____

_____

_____

_____

Daily Affirmation_____

Self-Care_____

MAKING SUCCESS A REALITY

Daily Affirmation_____

Self-Care_____

_____

_____

_____

_____

_____

_____

_____

_____

_____

_____

_____

_____

Daily Affirmation_____

Self-Care_____

MAKING SUCCESS A REALITY

Daily Affirmation _____

Self-Care _____

Daily Affirmation_____

Self-Care_____

MAKING SUCCESS A REALITY

Daily Affirmation_____

Self-Care_____

Daily Affirmation_____

Self-Care_____

MAKING SUCCESS A REALITY

Daily Affirmation_____

Self-Care_____

_____

_____

_____

_____

_____

_____

_____

_____

_____

_____

_____

_____

_____

Daily Affirmation_____

Self-Care_____

MAKING SUCCESS A REALITY

Daily Affirmation_____

Self-Care_____

Daily Affirmation_____

Self-Care_____

MAKING SUCCESS A REALITY

Daily Affirmation_____

Self-Care_____

_____

_____

_____

_____

_____

_____

_____

_____

_____

_____

_____

_____

_____

Daily Affirmation_____

Self-Care_____

_____

_____

_____

_____

_____

_____

_____

_____

_____

_____

_____

_____

_____

MAKING SUCCESS A REALITY

Daily Affirmation_____

Self-Care_____

_____

_____

_____

_____

_____

_____

_____

_____

_____

_____

_____

_____

Daily Affirmation_____

Self-Care_____

MAKING SUCCESS A REALITY

Daily Affirmation_____

Self-Care_____

_____

_____

_____

_____

_____

_____

_____

_____

_____

_____

_____

_____

_____

Daily Affirmation_____

Self-Care_____

MAKING SUCCESS A REALITY

Daily Affirmation_____

Self-Care_____

_____

_____

_____

_____

_____

_____

_____

_____

_____

_____

_____

_____

Daily Affirmation_____

Self-Care_____

MAKING SUCCESS A REALITY

Daily Affirmation_____

Self-Care_____

_____

_____

_____

_____

_____

_____

_____

_____

_____

_____

_____

_____

_____

_____

Daily Affirmation_____

Self-Care_____

_____

_____

_____

_____

_____

_____

_____

_____

_____

_____

_____

_____

_____

MAKING SUCCESS A REALITY

Daily Affirmation_____

Self-Care_____

_____

_____

_____

_____

_____

_____

_____

_____

_____

_____

_____

_____

Daily Affirmation_____

Self-Care_____

MAKING SUCCESS A REALITY

Daily Affirmation_____

Self-Care_____

_____

_____

_____

_____

_____

_____

_____

_____

_____

_____

_____

_____

_____

Daily Affirmation_____

Self-Care_____

MAKING SUCCESS A REALITY

Daily Affirmation_____

Self-Care_____

_____

_____

_____

_____

_____

_____

_____

_____

_____

_____

_____

_____

Daily Affirmation_____

Self-Care_____

MAKING SUCCESS A REALITY

Daily Affirmation_____

Self-Care_____

_____

_____

_____

_____

_____

_____

_____

_____

_____

_____

_____

_____

_____

Daily Affirmation_____

Self-Care_____

MAKING SUCCESS A REALITY

Daily Affirmation_____

Self-Care_____

Daily Affirmation_____

Self-Care_____

MAKING SUCCESS A REALITY

Daily Affirmation_____

Self-Care_____

_____

_____

_____

_____

_____

_____

_____

_____

_____

_____

_____

_____

Daily Affirmation_____

Self-Care_____

MAKING SUCCESS A REALITY

Daily Affirmation_____

Self-Care_____

Daily Affirmation_____

Self-Care_____

MAKING SUCCESS A REALITY

Daily Affirmation_____

Self-Care_____

_____

_____

_____

_____

_____

_____

_____

_____

_____

_____

_____

_____

_____

Daily Affirmation_____

Self-Care_____

MAKING SUCCESS A REALITY

Daily Affirmation_____

Self-Care_____

_____

_____

_____

_____

_____

_____

_____

_____

_____

_____

_____

_____

_____

Daily Affirmation_____

Self-Care_____

MAKING SUCCESS A REALITY

Daily Affirmation_____

Self-Care_____

Daily Affirmation_____

Self-Care_____

MAKING SUCCESS A REALITY

Daily Affirmation_____

Self-Care_____

Daily Affirmation_____

Self-Care_____

MAKING SUCCESS A REALITY

Daily Affirmation _____

Self-Care _____

_____

_____

_____

_____

_____

_____

_____

_____

_____

_____

_____

_____

_____

Daily Affirmation_____

Self-Care_____

_____

_____

_____

_____

_____

_____

_____

_____

_____

_____

_____

_____

_____

MAKING SUCCESS A REALITY

Daily Affirmation_____

Self-Care_____

_____

_____

_____

_____

_____

_____

_____

_____

_____

_____

_____

_____

Daily Affirmation_____

Self-Care_____

MAKING SUCCESS A REALITY

Daily Affirmation_____

Self-Care_____

_____

_____

_____

_____

_____

_____

_____

_____

_____

_____

_____

_____

Daily Affirmation_____

Self-Care_____

MAKING SUCCESS A REALITY

Daily Affirmation_____

Self-Care_____

_____

_____

_____

_____

_____

_____

_____

_____

_____

_____

_____

_____

_____

Daily Affirmation_____

Self-Care_____

MAKING SUCCESS A REALITY

Daily Affirmation_____

Self-Care_____

Daily Affirmation_____

Self-Care_____

MAKING SUCCESS A REALITY

Daily Affirmation_____

Self-Care_____

_____

_____

_____

_____

_____

_____

_____

_____

_____

_____

_____

_____

Daily Affirmation_____

Self-Care_____

MAKING SUCCESS A REALITY

Daily Affirmation_____

Self-Care_____

_____

_____

_____

_____

_____

_____

_____

_____

_____

_____

_____

_____

Daily Affirmation_____

Self-Care_____

_____

_____

_____

_____

_____

_____

_____

_____

_____

_____

_____

_____

_____

MAKING SUCCESS A REALITY

Daily Affirmation_____

Self-Care_____

_____

_____

_____

_____

_____

_____

_____

_____

_____

_____

_____

_____

Daily Affirmation_____

Self-Care_____

MAKING SUCCESS A REALITY

Daily Affirmation_____

Self-Care_____

_____

_____

_____

_____

_____

_____

_____

_____

_____

_____

_____

_____

Daily Affirmation_____

Self-Care_____

MAKING SUCCESS A REALITY

Daily Affirmation _____

Self-Care _____

_____

_____

_____

_____

_____

_____

_____

_____

_____

_____

_____

_____

_____

Daily Affirmation_____

Self-Care_____

MAKING SUCCESS A REALITY

Daily Affirmation_____

Self-Care_____

_____

_____

_____

_____

_____

_____

_____

_____

_____

_____

_____

_____

_____

Daily Affirmation_____

Self-Care_____

MAKING SUCCESS A REALITY

Daily Affirmation_____

Self-Care_____

Daily Affirmation_____

Self-Care_____

_____

_____

_____

_____

_____

_____

_____

_____

_____

_____

_____

_____

_____

MAKING SUCCESS A REALITY

Daily Affirmation_____

Self-Care_____

_____

_____

_____

_____

_____

_____

_____

_____

_____

_____

_____

_____

_____

Daily Affirmation_____

Self-Care_____

MAKING SUCCESS A REALITY

Daily Affirmation_____

Self-Care_____

_____

_____

_____

_____

_____

_____

_____

_____

_____

_____

_____

Daily Affirmation_____

Self-Care_____

MAKING SUCCESS A REALITY

Daily Affirmation _____

Self-Care _____

_____

_____

_____

_____

_____

_____

_____

_____

_____

_____

_____

_____

_____

_____

Daily Affirmation_____

Self-Care_____

MAKING SUCCESS A REALITY

Daily Affirmation_____

Self-Care_____

_____

_____

_____

_____

_____

_____

_____

_____

_____

_____

_____

_____

Daily Affirmation_____

Self-Care_____

MAKING SUCCESS A REALITY

Daily Affirmation_____

Self-Care_____

Daily Affirmation_____

Self-Care_____

MAKING SUCCESS A REALITY

Daily Affirmation_____

Self-Care_____

_____

_____

_____

_____

_____

_____

_____

_____

_____

_____

_____

_____

_____

Daily Affirmation_____

Self-Care_____

MAKING SUCCESS A REALITY

Daily Affirmation_____

Self-Care_____

_____

_____

_____

_____

_____

_____

_____

_____

_____

_____

_____

_____

_____

Daily Affirmation_____

Self-Care_____

MAKING SUCCESS A REALITY

Daily Affirmation_____

Self-Care_____

Daily Affirmation_____

Self-Care_____

MAKING SUCCESS A REALITY

Daily Affirmation_____

Self-Care_____

_____

_____

_____

_____

_____

_____

_____

_____

_____

_____

_____

_____

_____

_____

Daily Affirmation_____

Self-Care_____

MAKING SUCCESS A REALITY

Daily Affirmation_____

Self-Care_____

_____

_____

_____

_____

_____

_____

_____

_____

_____

_____

_____

_____

_____

Daily Affirmation_____

Self-Care_____

MAKING SUCCESS A REALITY

Daily Affirmation_____

Self-Care_____

_____

_____

_____

_____

_____

_____

_____

_____

_____

_____

_____

_____

_____

Daily Affirmation_____

Self-Care_____

MAKING SUCCESS A REALITY

Daily Affirmation_____

Self-Care_____

Daily Affirmation_____

Self-Care_____

MAKING SUCCESS A REALITY

Daily Affirmation_____

Self-Care_____

Daily Affirmation_____

Self-Care_____

MAKING SUCCESS A REALITY

Daily Affirmation_____

Self-Care_____

Daily Affirmation_____

Self-Care_____

MAKING SUCCESS A REALITY

Daily Affirmation_____

Self-Care_____

_____

_____

_____

_____

_____

_____

_____

_____

_____

_____

_____

_____

_____

_____

Daily Affirmation_____

Self-Care_____

MAKING SUCCESS A REALITY

Daily Affirmation_____

Self-Care_____

_____

_____

_____

_____

_____

_____

_____

_____

_____

_____

_____

_____

_____

Daily Affirmation_____

Self-Care_____

MAKING SUCCESS A REALITY

Daily Affirmation_____

Self-Care_____

_____

_____

_____

_____

_____

_____

_____

_____

_____

_____

_____

_____

Daily Affirmation_____

Self-Care_____

MAKING SUCCESS A REALITY

Daily Affirmation_____

Self-Care_____

_____

_____

_____

_____

_____

_____

_____

_____

_____

_____

_____

_____

Daily Affirmation_____

Self-Care_____

MAKING SUCCESS A REALITY

Daily Affirmation_____

Self-Care_____

_____

_____

_____

_____

_____

_____

_____

_____

_____

_____

_____

_____

_____

Daily Affirmation_____

Self-Care_____

MAKING SUCCESS A REALITY

Daily Affirmation_____

Self-Care_____

_____

_____

_____

_____

_____

_____

_____

_____

_____

_____

_____

_____

_____

Daily Affirmation_____

Self-Care_____

MAKING SUCCESS A REALITY

Daily Affirmation _____

Self-Care _____

_____

_____

_____

_____

_____

_____

_____

_____

_____

_____

_____

_____

_____

Daily Affirmation_____

Self-Care_____

MAKING SUCCESS A REALITY

Daily Affirmation_____

Self-Care_____

_____

_____

_____

_____

_____

_____

_____

_____

_____

_____

_____

_____

_____

Daily Affirmation_____

Self-Care_____

MAKING SUCCESS A REALITY

Daily Affirmation_____

Self-Care_____

Daily Affirmation_____

Self-Care_____

MAKING SUCCESS A REALITY

Daily Affirmation_____

Self-Care_____

_____

_____

_____

_____

_____

_____

_____

_____

_____

_____

_____

_____

_____

Daily Affirmation_____

Self-Care_____

_____

_____

_____

_____

_____

_____

_____

_____

_____

_____

_____

_____

_____

MAKING SUCCESS A REALITY

Daily Affirmation_____

Self-Care_____

Daily Affirmation_____

Self-Care_____

MAKING SUCCESS A REALITY

Daily Affirmation_____

Self-Care_____

Daily Affirmation_____

Self-Care_____

MAKING SUCCESS A REALITY

Daily Affirmation_____

Self-Care_____

_____

_____

_____

_____

_____

_____

_____

_____

_____

_____

_____

_____

_____

Daily Affirmation_____

Self-Care_____

MAKING SUCCESS A REALITY

Daily Affirmation_____

Self-Care_____

Daily Affirmation_____

Self-Care_____

MAKING SUCCESS A REALITY

Daily Affirmation_____

Self-Care_____

Daily Affirmation_____

Self-Care_____

MAKING SUCCESS A REALITY

Daily Affirmation_____

Self-Care_____

_____

_____

_____

_____

_____

_____

_____

_____

_____

_____

_____

_____

Daily Affirmation_____

Self-Care_____

MAKING SUCCESS A REALITY

Daily Affirmation_____

Self-Care_____

_____

_____

_____

_____

_____

_____

_____

_____

_____

_____

_____

_____

Daily Affirmation_____

Self-Care_____

MAKING SUCCESS A REALITY

Daily Affirmation_____

Self-Care_____

Daily Affirmation_____

Self-Care_____

_____

_____

_____

_____

_____

_____

_____

_____

_____

_____

_____

_____

_____

MAKING SUCCESS A REALITY

Daily Affirmation_____

Self-Care_____

_____

_____

_____

_____

_____

_____

_____

_____

_____

_____

_____

_____

_____

_____

Daily Affirmation_____

Self-Care_____

MAKING SUCCESS A REALITY

Daily Affirmation_____

Self-Care_____

Daily Affirmation_____

Self-Care_____

MAKING SUCCESS A REALITY

Daily Affirmation_____

Self-Care_____

_____

_____

_____

_____

_____

_____

_____

_____

_____

_____

_____

_____

Daily Affirmation_____

Self-Care_____

MAKING SUCCESS A REALITY

Daily Affirmation_____

Self-Care_____

Daily Affirmation_____

Self-Care_____

_____

_____

_____

_____

_____

_____

_____

_____

_____

_____

_____

_____

MAKING SUCCESS A REALITY

Daily Affirmation_____

Self-Care_____

_____

_____

_____

_____

_____

_____

_____

_____

_____

_____

_____

_____

_____

Daily Affirmation_____

Self-Care_____

MAKING SUCCESS A REALITY

Daily Affirmation_____

Self-Care_____

_____

_____

_____

_____

_____

_____

_____

_____

_____

_____

_____

_____

_____

Daily Affirmation_____

Self-Care_____

MAKING SUCCESS A REALITY

Daily Affirmation_____

Self-Care_____

_____

_____

_____

_____

_____

_____

_____

_____

_____

_____

_____

_____

_____

Daily Affirmation_____

Self-Care_____

MAKING SUCCESS A REALITY

Daily Affirmation_____

Self-Care_____

Daily Affirmation_____

Self-Care_____

_____

_____

_____

_____

_____

_____

_____

_____

_____

_____

_____

_____

_____

MAKING SUCCESS A REALITY

Daily Affirmation_____

Self-Care_____

Daily Affirmation_____

Self-Care_____

MAKING SUCCESS A REALITY

Daily Affirmation_____

Self-Care_____

Daily Affirmation_____

Self-Care_____

MAKING SUCCESS A REALITY

Daily Affirmation_____

Self-Care_____

Daily Affirmation_____

Self-Care_____

MAKING SUCCESS A REALITY

Daily Affirmation_____

Self-Care_____

_____

_____

_____

_____

_____

_____

_____

_____

_____

_____

_____

_____

_____

Daily Affirmation_____

Self-Care_____

MAKING SUCCESS A REALITY

Daily Affirmation_____

Self-Care_____

_____

_____

_____

_____

_____

_____

_____

_____

_____

_____

_____

_____

_____

_____

Daily Affirmation_____

Self-Care_____

MAKING SUCCESS A REALITY

Daily Affirmation_____

Self-Care_____

Daily Affirmation_____

Self-Care_____

MAKING SUCCESS A REALITY

Daily Affirmation_____

Self-Care_____

Daily Affirmation_____

Self-Care_____

MAKING SUCCESS A REALITY

Daily Affirmation_____

Self-Care_____

_____

_____

_____

_____

_____

_____

_____

_____

_____

_____

_____

_____

Daily Affirmation_____

Self-Care_____

MAKING SUCCESS A REALITY

Daily Affirmation_____

Self-Care_____

Daily Affirmation_____

Self-Care_____

MAKING SUCCESS A REALITY

Daily Affirmation_____

Self-Care_____

Daily Affirmation_____

Self-Care_____

MAKING SUCCESS A REALITY

Daily Affirmation_____

Self-Care_____

_____

_____

_____

_____

_____

_____

_____

_____

_____

_____

_____

_____

Daily Affirmation_____

Self-Care_____

_____

_____

_____

_____

_____

_____

_____

_____

_____

_____

_____

_____

MAKING SUCCESS A REALITY

Daily Affirmation_____

Self-Care_____

_____

_____

_____

_____

_____

_____

_____

_____

_____

_____

_____

_____

_____

Daily Affirmation_____

Self-Care_____

MAKING SUCCESS A REALITY

Daily Affirmation_____

Self-Care_____

Daily Affirmation_____

Self-Care_____

MAKING SUCCESS A REALITY

Daily Affirmation_____

Self-Care_____

Daily Affirmation_____

Self-Care_____

MAKING SUCCESS A REALITY

Daily Affirmation _____

Self-Care _____

_____

_____

_____

_____

_____

_____

_____

_____

_____

_____

_____

_____

_____

Daily Affirmation_____

Self-Care_____

MAKING SUCCESS A REALITY

Daily Affirmation_____

Self-Care_____

Daily Affirmation_____

Self-Care_____

MAKING SUCCESS A REALITY

Daily Affirmation_____

Self-Care_____

Daily Affirmation_____

Self-Care_____

MAKING SUCCESS A REALITY

Daily Affirmation_____

Self-Care_____

_____

_____

_____

_____

_____

_____

_____

_____

_____

_____

_____

_____

Daily Affirmation_____

Self-Care_____

MAKING SUCCESS A REALITY

Daily Affirmation_____

Self-Care_____

Daily Affirmation_____

Self-Care_____

MAKING SUCCESS A REALITY

Daily Affirmation_____

Self-Care_____

Daily Affirmation_____

Self-Care_____

MAKING SUCCESS A REALITY

Daily Affirmation _____

Self-Care _____

_____

_____

_____

_____

_____

_____

_____

_____

_____

_____

_____

_____

_____

Daily Affirmation_____

Self-Care_____

MAKING SUCCESS A REALITY

Daily Affirmation_____

Self-Care_____

Daily Affirmation_____

Self-Care_____

MAKING SUCCESS A REALITY

Daily Affirmation_____

Self-Care_____

_____

_____

_____

_____

_____

_____

_____

_____

_____

_____

_____

_____

_____

Daily Affirmation_____

Self-Care_____

MAKING SUCCESS A REALITY

Daily Affirmation_____

Self-Care_____

Daily Affirmation_____

Self-Care_____

_____

_____

_____

_____

_____

_____

_____

_____

_____

_____

_____

_____

_____

MAKING SUCCESS A REALITY

Daily Affirmation _____

Self-Care _____

_____

_____

_____

_____

_____

_____

_____

_____

_____

_____

_____

_____

Daily Affirmation_____

Self-Care_____

MAKING SUCCESS A REALITY

Daily Affirmation_____

Self-Care_____

_____

_____

_____

_____

_____

_____

_____

_____

_____

_____

_____

_____

_____

Daily Affirmation_____

Self-Care_____

MAKING SUCCESS A REALITY

Daily Affirmation_____

Self-Care_____

Daily Affirmation_____

Self-Care_____

MAKING SUCCESS A REALITY

Daily Affirmation_____

Self-Care_____

Daily Affirmation_____

Self-Care_____

MAKING SUCCESS A REALITY

Daily Affirmation_____

Self-Care_____

Daily Affirmation_____

Self-Care_____

MAKING SUCCESS A REALITY

Daily Affirmation _____

Self-Care _____

Daily Affirmation_____

Self-Care_____

MAKING SUCCESS A REALITY

Daily Affirmation_____

Self-Care_____

_____

_____

_____

_____

_____

_____

_____

_____

_____

_____

_____

_____

_____

Daily Affirmation_____

Self-Care_____

MAKING SUCCESS A REALITY

Daily Affirmation_____

Self-Care_____

_____

_____

_____

_____

_____

_____

_____

_____

_____

_____

_____

_____

_____

_____

Daily Affirmation_____

Self-Care_____

MAKING SUCCESS A REALITY

Daily Affirmation_____

Self-Care_____

_____

_____

_____

_____

_____

_____

_____

_____

_____

_____

_____

_____

_____

Daily Affirmation_____

Self-Care_____

MAKING SUCCESS A REALITY

Daily Affirmation_____

Self-Care_____

Daily Affirmation_____

Self-Care_____

MAKING SUCCESS A REALITY

Daily Affirmation_____

Self-Care_____

_____

_____

_____

_____

_____

_____

_____

_____

_____

_____

_____

_____

_____

Daily Affirmation_____

Self-Care_____

MAKING SUCCESS A REALITY

Daily Affirmation_____

Self-Care_____

Daily Affirmation_____

Self-Care_____

MAKING SUCCESS A REALITY

Daily Affirmation_____

Self-Care_____

Daily Affirmation_____

Self-Care_____

MAKING SUCCESS A REALITY

Daily Affirmation _____

Self-Care _____

_____

_____

_____

_____

_____

_____

_____

_____

_____

_____

_____

_____

Daily Affirmation_____

Self-Care_____

MAKING SUCCESS A REALITY

Daily Affirmation_____

Self-Care_____

Daily Affirmation_____

Self-Care_____

MAKING SUCCESS A REALITY

Daily Affirmation_____

Self-Care_____

Daily Affirmation_____

Self-Care_____

MAKING SUCCESS A REALITY

Daily Affirmation_____

Self-Care_____

Daily Affirmation_____

Self-Care_____

MAKING SUCCESS A REALITY

Daily Affirmation_____

Self-Care_____

Daily Affirmation_____

Self-Care_____

MAKING SUCCESS A REALITY

Daily Affirmation _____

Self-Care _____

Daily Affirmation_____

Self-Care_____

MAKING SUCCESS A REALITY

Daily Affirmation_____

Self-Care_____

_____

_____

_____

_____

_____

_____

_____

_____

_____

_____

_____

Daily Affirmation_____

Self-Care_____

MAKING SUCCESS A REALITY

Daily Affirmation_____

Self-Care_____

_____

_____

_____

_____

_____

_____

_____

_____

_____

_____

_____

_____

_____

Daily Affirmation_____

Self-Care_____

_____

_____

_____

_____

_____

_____

_____

_____

_____

_____

_____

_____

_____

_____

MAKING SUCCESS A REALITY

Daily Affirmation_____

Self-Care_____

Daily Affirmation_____

Self-Care_____

_____

_____

_____

_____

_____

_____

_____

_____

_____

_____

_____

_____

_____

MAKING SUCCESS A REALITY

Daily Affirmation_____

Self-Care_____

Daily Affirmation_____

Self-Care_____

MAKING SUCCESS A REALITY

Daily Affirmation_____

Self-Care_____

Daily Affirmation_____

Self-Care_____

MAKING SUCCESS A REALITY

Daily Affirmation_____

Self-Care_____

Daily Affirmation_____

Self-Care_____

Daily Affirmation_____

Self-Care_____

Daily Affirmation_____

Self-Care_____

MAKING SUCCESS A REALITY

Daily Affirmation _____

Self-Care _____

Daily Affirmation_____

Self-Care_____

MAKING SUCCESS A REALITY

Daily Affirmation_____

Self-Care_____

Daily Affirmation_____

Self-Care_____

MAKING SUCCESS A REALITY

Daily Affirmation _____

Self-Care _____

_____

_____

_____

_____

_____

_____

_____

_____

_____

_____

_____

_____

_____

_____

Daily Affirmation_____

Self-Care_____

MAKING SUCCESS A REALITY

Daily Affirmation _____

Self-Care _____

Daily Affirmation_____

Self-Care_____

MAKING SUCCESS A REALITY

Daily Affirmation_____

Self-Care_____

Daily Affirmation_____

Self-Care_____

MAKING SUCCESS A REALITY

Daily Affirmation_____

Self-Care_____

Daily Affirmation_____

Self-Care_____

_____

_____

_____

_____

_____

_____

_____

_____

_____

_____

_____

_____

_____

MAKING SUCCESS A REALITY

Daily Affirmation_____

Self-Care_____

_____

_____

_____

_____

_____

_____

_____

_____

_____

_____

_____

_____

_____

Daily Affirmation_____

Self-Care_____

MAKING SUCCESS A REALITY

Daily Affirmation_____

Self-Care_____

Daily Affirmation_____

Self-Care_____

MAKING SUCCESS A REALITY

Daily Affirmation_____

Self-Care_____

_____

_____

_____

_____

_____

_____

_____

_____

_____

_____

_____

_____

_____

Daily Affirmation_____

Self-Care_____

_____

_____

_____

_____

_____

_____

_____

_____

_____

_____

_____

_____

MAKING SUCCESS A REALITY

Daily Affirmation_____

Self-Care_____

_____

_____

_____

_____

_____

_____

_____

_____

_____

_____

_____

_____

_____

Daily Affirmation_____

Self-Care_____

MAKING SUCCESS A REALITY

Daily Affirmation_____

Self-Care_____

Daily Affirmation_____

Self-Care_____

MAKING SUCCESS A REALITY

Daily Affirmation_____

Self-Care_____

Daily Affirmation_____

Self-Care_____

MAKING SUCCESS A REALITY

Daily Affirmation_____

Self-Care_____

Daily Affirmation_____

Self-Care_____

MAKING SUCCESS A REALITY

Daily Affirmation_____

Self-Care_____

Daily Affirmation_____

Self-Care_____

MAKING SUCCESS A REALITY

Daily Affirmation_____

Self-Care_____

Daily Affirmation_____

Self-Care_____

MAKING SUCCESS A REALITY

Daily Affirmation _____

Self-Care _____

Daily Affirmation_____

Self-Care_____

_____

_____

_____

_____

_____

_____

_____

_____

_____

_____

_____

_____

_____

MAKING SUCCESS A REALITY

Daily Affirmation_____

Self-Care_____

Daily Affirmation_____

Self-Care_____

MAKING SUCCESS A REALITY

Daily Affirmation_____

Self-Care_____

_____

_____

_____

_____

_____

_____

_____

_____

_____

_____

_____

_____

Daily Affirmation_____

Self-Care_____

MAKING SUCCESS A REALITY

Daily Affirmation_____

Self-Care_____

Daily Affirmation_____

Self-Care_____

MAKING SUCCESS A REALITY

Daily Affirmation_____

Self-Care_____

Daily Affirmation_____

Self-Care_____

MAKING SUCCESS A REALITY

Daily Affirmation_____

Self-Care_____

_____

_____

_____

_____

_____

_____

_____

_____

_____

_____

_____

_____

_____

Daily Affirmation_____

Self-Care_____

MAKING SUCCESS A REALITY

Daily Affirmation_____

Self-Care_____

_____

_____

_____

_____

_____

_____

_____

_____

_____

_____

_____

_____

Daily Affirmation_____

Self-Care_____

_____

_____

_____

_____

_____

_____

_____

_____

_____

_____

_____

_____

_____

MAKING SUCCESS A REALITY

Daily Affirmation_____

Self-Care_____

_____

_____

_____

_____

_____

_____

_____

_____

_____

_____

_____

_____

_____

Daily Affirmation_____

Self-Care_____

MAKING SUCCESS A REALITY

Daily Affirmation_____

Self-Care_____

Daily Affirmation_____

Self-Care_____

MAKING SUCCESS A REALITY

Daily Affirmation_____

Self-Care_____

Daily Affirmation_____

Self-Care_____

MAKING SUCCESS A REALITY

Daily Affirmation _____

Self-Care _____

_____

_____

_____

_____

_____

_____

_____

_____

_____

_____

_____

_____

_____

Daily Affirmation_____

Self-Care_____

_____

_____

_____

_____

_____

_____

_____

_____

_____

_____

_____

_____

_____

_____

MAKING SUCCESS A REALITY

Daily Affirmation_____

Self-Care_____

_____

_____

_____

_____

_____

_____

_____

_____

_____

_____

_____

_____

Daily Affirmation_____

Self-Care_____

MAKING SUCCESS A REALITY

Daily Affirmation_____

Self-Care_____

_____

_____

_____

_____

_____

_____

_____

_____

_____

_____

_____

_____

Daily Affirmation_____

Self-Care_____

_____

_____

_____

_____

_____

_____

_____

_____

_____

_____

_____

_____

_____

MAKING SUCCESS A REALITY

Daily Affirmation _____

Self-Care _____

_____

_____

_____

_____

_____

_____

_____

_____

_____

_____

_____

_____

_____

Daily Affirmation_____

Self-Care_____

MAKING SUCCESS A REALITY

Daily Affirmation_____

Self-Care_____

Daily Affirmation_____

Self-Care_____

MAKING SUCCESS A REALITY

Daily Affirmation_____

Self-Care_____

_____

_____

_____

_____

_____

_____

_____

_____

_____

_____

_____

_____

_____

_____

Daily Affirmation_____

Self-Care_____

About the Author

Melissa S. Myers is the author of "Making Success A Reality, Success Journal", Business Owner, Community Leader, and Philanthropist.

Melissa has dedicated her life to helping others achieve dreams that were thought to be unachievable. With that Melissa has instructed courses and led seminars that allow those seeking change to create a life of abundance by providing the necessary tools and guidance.

Melissa believes that her selfless nature and spiritual belief has developed her own personal growth and blessings to overflow in her life, as she believes that we all have control over our destiny.

For more information about Melissa S. Myers visit melissasmyers.com.

www.ingramcontent.com/pod-product-compliance
Lightning Source LLC
Chambersburg PA
CBHW060303010526
44108CB00042B/2615